George Müller

Does money grow on trees?

The true story of George Müller
and the hidden coins
Catherine Mackenzie
Illustrated by Rita Ammassari

'Does money grow on trees?' a friend asked George Müller one day. 'You spend so much of it, perhaps it does?'

George laughed as he climbed up a nearby apple tree. 'Germany has the best trees in the world,' he declared. 'Unfortunately money doesn't grow on any of them.'

George still spent lots of money though. He spent what he did not have on things that he did not need and then he stole more money to buy even more things. George even stole money from his father's desk.

George laughed as he climbed
up a nearby apple tree.

When George's father counted his money he noticed that some was missing. He didn't trust George so he looked in the boy's pockets. There was nothing there. Then he told George to take off his shoes. That was where George had hidden the coins. George's father was very disappointed. His son was a thief.

However, George was not sorry for what he had done. He carried on stealing and finally he was thrown in prison.

George's father was very
disappointed. His son was a thief.

When George got out of prison he still did not feel sorry. He did not feel sorry one bit. He kept on cheating and stealing and telling lies to his father. He even stole money from his friends at school.

One of George's friends started to read the Bible. 'Why do you read that book? What are these meetings you go to?' George asked. 'Can I come with you?'

One of George's friends started to read the Bible.

The people at the meetings were very happy and friendly. 'I would love to be just like them,' George thought. 'I am always wishing for things that I don't have. I keep stealing in order to get them. I pretend I feel great but I really feel miserable.'

George listened to someone pray and then he asked God to forgive him for his sins. George asked Jesus to be his Saviour. George's life was changed forever.

The people at the meetings were very
happy and friendly.

Some of George's friends weren't pleased when he became a Christian. 'He's no fun anymore,' they complained. George's father wasn't pleased either. 'I have spent a lot of money on your education. I don't want you to become a missionary!' he yelled. But George did not change his mind. He knew what Jesus wanted him to do. 'A missionary works for God. I will work for God. God will give me everything I need,' George said. 'I can trust in him. I know I can.'

'God will give me everything I need,'
George said. 'I can trust in him.
I know I can.'

George went to England and met a young woman called Mary. They fell in love.

'Will you marry me?' he asked her. She said yes. They both wanted to work for God together. God looked after them.

One day there was no food in the house and George had no money. Just then they found some meat and bread had been left on their doorstep. 'God gave it to us,' exclaimed Mary. 'We can trust in him. I know we can!'

George met a young woman called Mary.
'Will you marry me?' he asked her.

George and Mary set up home in Bristol but soon the disease of cholera spread through the city. Many people died. However, when God took the cholera away many in the city began to come to church. They wanted to learn about the love of Jesus. George started special schools to teach everyone about how God had sent his only Son to save people from their sins. The people longed to hear this really good news.

George needed a lot of help to do all that he had to do, but he knew that God was with him.

'God will give us the money we need,' George said. 'We can trust in him. I know we can.'

Many people came to church. They wanted to learn about the love of Jesus.

George was right. God always helped them even when sad times came. They were so upset when their baby boy died but they knew he was safe with Jesus. They also knew that many children in Bristol had no one to look after them. So George started an orphanage.

Some people thought he was mad. 'Where will you get the money?' they exclaimed.

'God will help me,' said George. 'I can trust in him. I know I can.'

There were many children in Bristol
who had no one to look after them.

George was right. God gave them all they needed. One lady sent forks, another sent a jug, someone else sent furniture. People sent money, food, clothes and shoes. God made sure that the Müllers got exactly the right things. Soon the first orphanage was ready but then a second and a third orphanage were needed. Where would they get the money?

'We can trust in God,' George declared. 'I know we can.'

People sent money, food,
clothes and shoes.

George was right. God always helped them. One day George needed an extra penny for bread. Just then a lady came and gave George two whole pennies. When the heating broke down in winter the builders agreed to work without stopping until it was mended. Just as the builders began to work the weather changed from winter to spring until the job was done. A little girl ran up to George laughing. 'Isn't it wonderful! We can trust in God. I know we can!'

The weather changed from winter to
spring until the job was done.

One morning George saw some orphans playing under an apple tree. 'Money does not grow on trees,' George thought to himself, 'but I used to behave as if it did.'

George Müller remembered stealing his father's coins. He was glad that God had taught him a lesson. 'God taught me to love Jesus and to trust in him for all my needs. Looking after all these children is difficult – but I can trust God to help me. I know I can.'

God taught George to love Jesus and
to trust in him for all his needs.

For Philip and Jack
With love and prayers that you too
will trust in the Lord Jesus.

© Copyright 2005 Catherine Mackenzie
Reprinted 2008 and 2012
ISBN: 978-1-84550-110-5
Published by Christian Focus Publications
Geanies House, Fearn, Tain, Ross-shire, IV20 1TW, Scotland, U.K.
www.christianfocus.com
Cover design by Daniel van Straaten
Printed in China
Other titles in this series:
Corrie ten Boom: Are all of the watches safe? 978-1-84550-109-9
Amy Carmichael: Can brown eyes be made blue? 978-1-84550-108-2
David Livingstone: Who is the bravest? 978-1-84550-384-0
Helen Roseveare: What's in the parcel? 978-1-84550-383-3
Hudson Taylor: Could somebody pass the salt? 978-1-84550-111-2